LEGO

THE KRISTIANSEN FAMILY

Lee Slater

Big Buddy Books

An Imprint of Abdo Publishing
abdobooks.com

abdobooks.com

Published by Abdo Publishing, a division of ABDO, PO Box 398166, Minneapolis, Minnesota 55439. Copyright © 2022 by Abdo Consulting Group, Inc. International copyrights reserved in all countries. No part of this book may be reproduced in any form without written permission from the publisher. Big Buddy Books™ is a trademark and logo of Abdo Publishing.

Printed in the United States of America, North Mankato, Minnesota
102021
012022

Design: Emily O'Malley, Mighty Media, Inc.
Production: Mighty Media, Inc.
Editor: Liz Salzmann
Cover Photographs: Bored Photography/Shutterstock Images (LEGOs), CAMAY SUNGU/AP Images (Kristiansen), Levent Konuk/Shutterstock Images (dinosaur, LEGO car), zaidi razak/Shutterstock Images (blue spaceman & Vader, LEGO man)
Interior Photographs: Alexis DUCLOS/Getty Images, p. 7; Baloncici/Shutterstock Images, p. 13; Bored Photography/Shutterstock Images, p. 28 (bottom); CAMAY SUNGU/AP Images, p. 19; Courtesy of The Strong®, Rochester, New York, pp. 17, 29 (bottom); David Mellis/Flickr, pp. 11, 28 (top right); Ekaterina_Minaeva/Shutterstock Images, p. 9; Frank Bach/Shutterstock Images, pp. 5, 28 (top left); Lester Balajadia/Shutterstock Images, p. 21; Levent Konuk/Shutterstock Images, p. 29 (top); Luigi Rosa/Flickr, p. 25; Matt Alexander/AP Images, p. 23; MeskPhotography/Shutterstock Images, p. 27; ovbelov/Shutterstock Images, p. 15

Library of Congress Control Number: 2021942806

Publisher's Cataloging-in-Publication Data
Names: Slater, Lee, author.
Title: LEGO: the Kristiansen family / by Lee Slater
Description: Minneapolis, Minnesota : Abdo Publishing, 2022 | Series: Toy stories | Includes online resources and index.
Identifiers: ISBN 9781532197116 (lib. bdg.) | ISBN 9781098219246 (ebook)
Subjects: LCSH: Kirk Christiansen, Ole, 1891-1958--Juvenile literature. | LEGO toys--Juvenile literature. | Inventors--Juvenile literature. | Toys--Juvenile literature. | LEGO koncernen (Denmark)--Juvenile literature.
Classification: DDC 338.47688--dc23

CONTENTS

CHAPTER 1

OLE KIRK CHRISTIANSEN

Ole Kirk Christiansen was born in Filskov, Denmark, on April 7, 1891. His parents were Jens and Kirstine Christiansen. Ole had nine **siblings**. Jens worked as a farmer.

Farming was one of
Denmark's largest
industries when Ole
was growing up.

OLE GROWS UP

Ole became a **carpenter**. He worked in Germany and Norway. In 1912, he married Kirstine Sorensen.

In 1916, Ole and Kirstine settled in Billund, Denmark. Ole started a carpentry business. He built homes and made furniture. The couple had four sons. Sadly, Kirstine died in 1932.

Godtfred Christiansen was Ole's third son. He eventually became the company's president.

CHAPTER 3

HARD TIMES

Ole's business suffered during the **Great Depression**. People had less money for homes and furniture. But they still wanted to make their children happy. So, Ole started making toys.

In 1935, Ole created the **brand** name LEGO for his toys. That same year, Ole married Sofie Jorgensen. In 1935, they had a daughter, Ulla.

Ole's woodworking skills made LEGO possible!

CHAPTER 4

THE FIRST LEGOS

Ole named his toy company the LEGO Group. By 1936, the company was making more than 40 different toys. The toys were very popular. In 1942, Ole stopped building homes and furniture. The LEGO Group began only making toys.

A duck on wheels was one of the most popular original LEGO toys.

CHAPTER 5

PLASTIC BEGINNINGS

The original LEGO toys were made of wood. In 1947, the LEGO Group bought an **injection molding machine**. The company started making plastic toys.

Two years later, LEGO began making plastic building blocks. They were called **Automatic** Binding Bricks. In 1953, they were renamed LEGO Bricks.

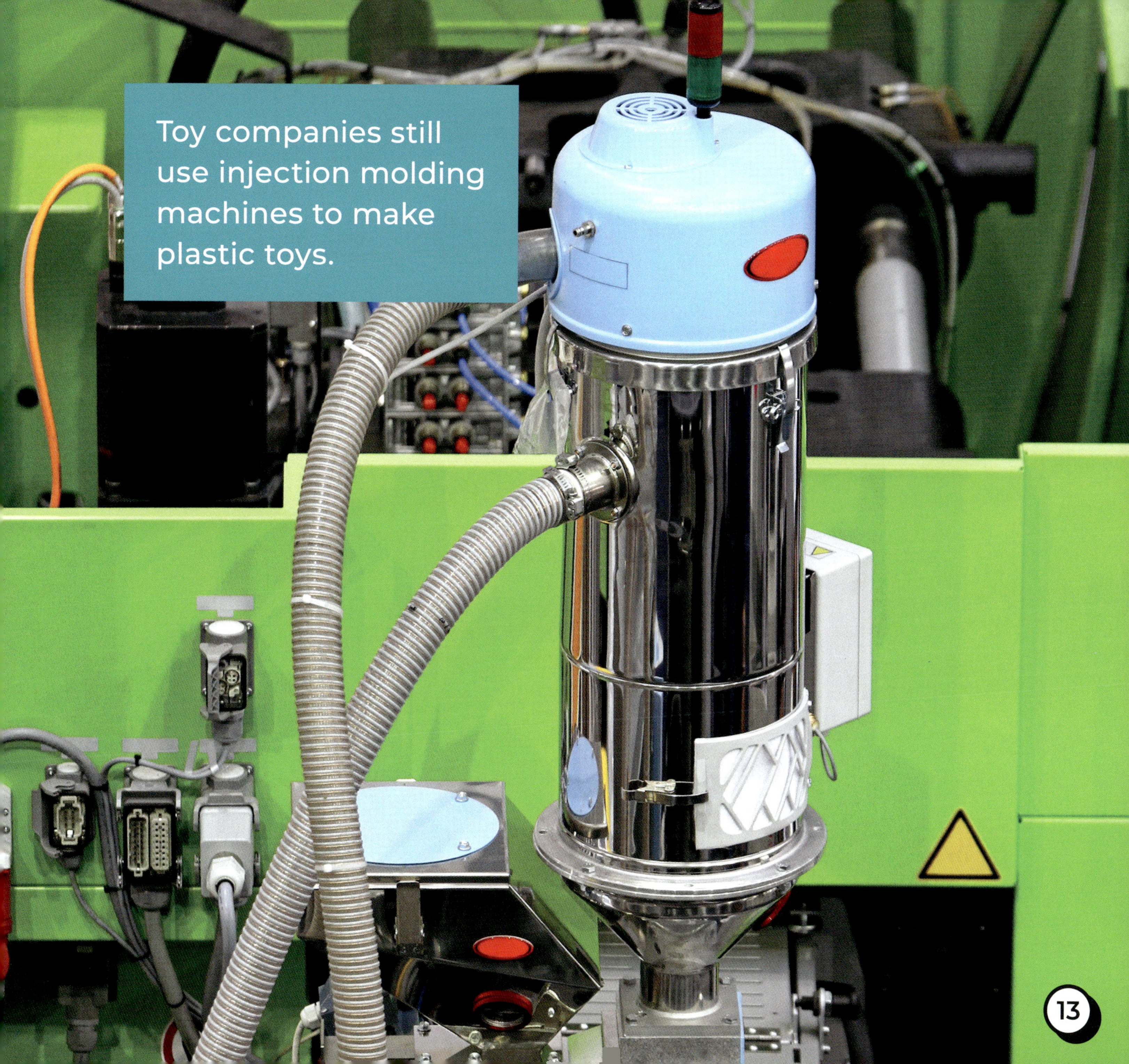

Toy companies still
use injection molding
machines to make
plastic toys.

LEGO BRICKS

Today, there are five main LEGO factories. Each one is in a different country. The factories have special machines that make the LEGO Bricks. Then, workers pack the LEGOs in boxes.

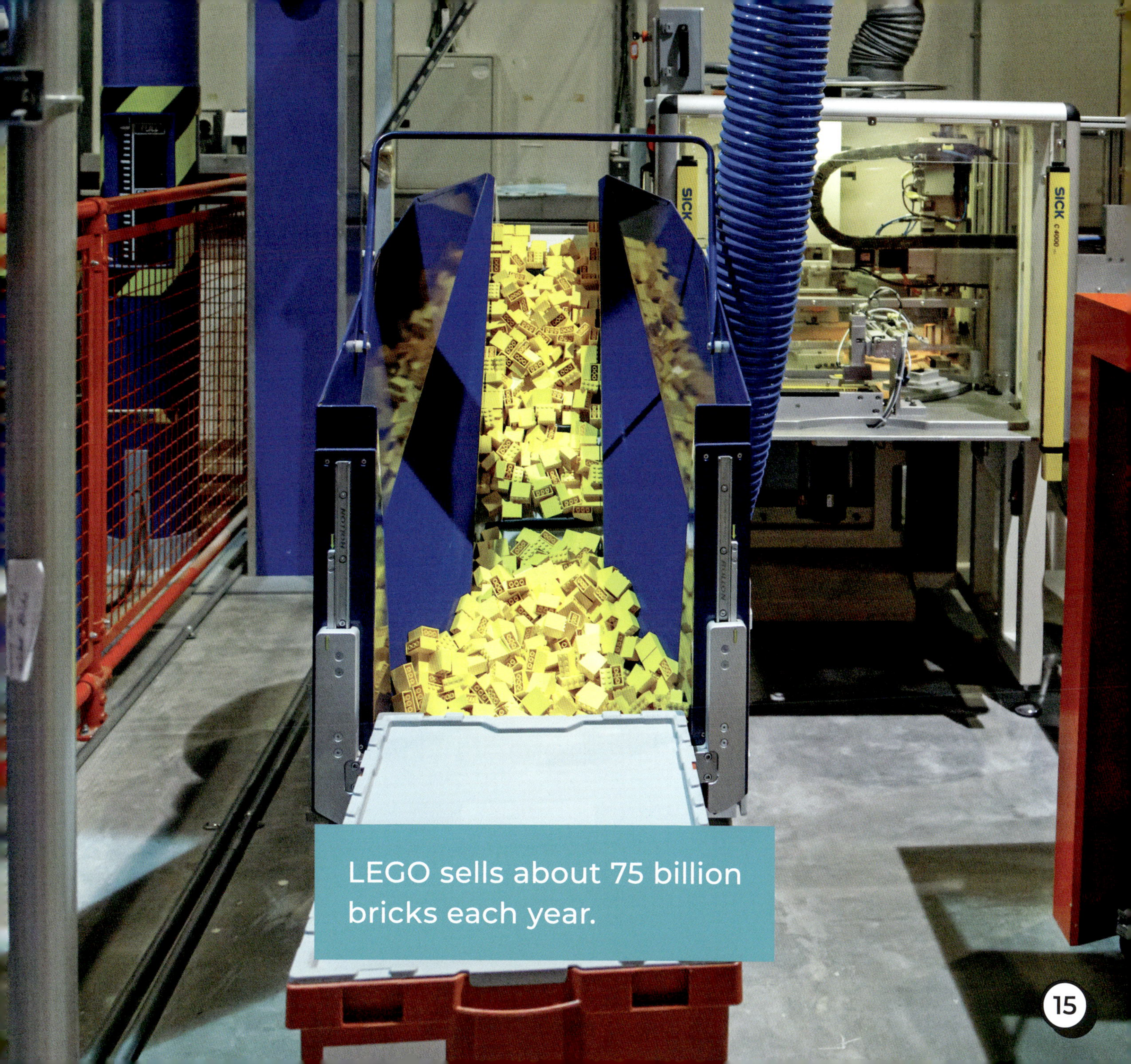

LEGO sells about 75 billion bricks each year.

 LEGO SYSTEMS

In 1955, LEGO began selling its System in Play. These were kits of LEGO Bricks that could be used together.

Three years later, LEGO improved the LEGO Brick **design**. The bottoms of the new bricks had three tubes inside them. This helped the bricks stick together.

The first System in Play kits let kids create their own towns.

CHAPTER 8

FAMILY BUSINESS

Ole Christiansen died on March 11, 1958. His son Godtfred became the company's president. Godtfred started **exporting** LEGO toys around the world.

Each **generation** of the family increased the company's success. This continued when Godtfred's son, Kjeld Kirk Kristiansen, took over as president in 1979.

Today, most family members, including Kjeld (*pictured*), spell their last name Kristiansen.

CHAPTER 9

GAME CHANGER

In the 1990s, video games were becoming popular. Many kids were less interested in toys like LEGOs. By 2004, the LEGO Group was losing money.

Kjeld knew it was time for a change. He hired Jørgen Vig Knudstorp to lead the company. Knudstorp was the first non-family member to be president.

There are ten LEGOLAND parks around the world.

CHAPTER 10

REBUILDING LEGO

As president, it was Knudstorp's job to make the company earn money again. Knudstorp **eliminated** products that cost too much or didn't sell well.

But what would cause kids to choose LEGOs over computer games? The LEGO Group needed to understand how modern kids played. So, they created the **Future** Lab.

Knudstorp wanted LEGO "to compete not by being the biggest but by being the best."

LEGO IDEAS

The **Future** Lab was a group of **researchers** and **designers**. Its job was to invent fun new LEGO products.

To help in this effort, Future Lab created LEGO Ideas to get input from fans. Anyone who is at least 13 years old can submit a design idea at the LEGO Ideas website. If enough other fans like the idea, LEGO considers developing it!

LEGO
IDEAS
INTERNATIONAL SPACE STATION SET
NATIONAL SPACE STATION SET
16+
21321
INTERNATIONAL SPACE STATION
The LEGO International Space Station kit was developed from a LEGO Ideas submission.
25

CHAPTER 12

THE FAMILY TODAY

Ole's strong **work ethic** guided the Kristiansens to great success. Today, Ole's **descendants** are among the wealthiest people in Denmark.

The Kristiansen family works to make a positive difference. LEGO toys continue to delight children all over the world. As Ole always said, "Only the best is good enough."

The LEGO Group
recycles more than
90 percent of its
production waste.

TIMELINE

1891

Ole Kirk Christiansen is born in Filskov, Denmark, on April 7.

1916

Ole opens a carpentry business.

1932

Ole's wife, Kirstine, dies.

1934

Ole marries Sofie Jorgensen. He creates the LEGO name.

1942

The LEGO Group begins to make only toys.

1949

The first Automatic Binding Bricks are produced.

1958

Ole dies. His son Godtfred Christiansen becomes company president.

2004

Jørgen Vig Knudstorp becomes company president.

1953

Automatic Binding Bricks are renamed LEGO Bricks.

1979

Godtfred's son Kjeld Kirk Kristiansen becomes company president.

29

GLOSSARY

automatic—moving or acting by itself.

brand—a category of products made by a particular company and all having the same company name.

carpentry—the trade of making or fixing wooden objects or building parts. A person who does carpentry is a carpenter.

descendant (dih-SEHN-duhnt)—a member of the same family.

design (dih-ZINE)—a plan for how something will appear or work. A designer is a person who plans how something will appear or work.

eliminate—to get rid of or remove.

export—to send goods to another country for sale.

future (FYOO-chuhr)—a time that has not yet occurred.

generation (jeh-nuh-RAY-shuhn)—a single step in the history of a family.

Great Depression—the period from 1929 to 1942 of worldwide economic trouble. There was little buying or selling, and many people could not find work.

injection molding machine—a machine that melts small pieces of plastic and feeds the melted plastic into molds to make new plastic objects.

researcher—a person who carefully studies a subject in order to learn facts about it.

sibling—a brother or a sister.

work ethic—the principle that hard work is valuable and worthy of reward.

ONLINE RESOURCES

To learn more about LEGO and the Kristiansen family, please visit **abdobooklinks.com** or scan this QR code. These links are routinely monitored and updated to provide the most current information available.

INDEX